Heartbreak: A Journey of Healing & Strength

How Black Men Heal

By Marlon BaCote MA, QMHP, CSAC, RPRS

Dedication

To every Black man who has felt unheard, and to every loved one who stood by in silence.

This book is for you.

May it bring light, healing, and hope.

Outline

1. **Introduction: Breaking the Silence**

    a. Purpose of the book.

    b. Personal story and context.

    c. Addressing the silence Black men face.

2. **Chapter 1: Understanding Heartbreak**

    a. The emotional, physical, and mental toll.

    b. Layers of heartbreak and generational wounds.

    c. Personal experiences with depression and trauma.

3. **Chapter 2: Steps Toward Healing**

    a. Acknowledging the pain.

    b. Finding support and embracing therapy.

Introduction: Breaking the Silence

For generations, Black men have carried an invisible weight—an unspoken burden shaped by systemic inequities, fractured family structures, and the pressures of a world that too often denies them the space to grieve, to heal, and to be vulnerable. This weight doesn't just exist in moments of tragedy or heartbreak; it is a daily reality that shapes how we see ourselves and how the world sees us.

Heartbreak is one of the most isolated experiences we face. It's not just the loss of love—it's the loss of identity, stability, and connection. For Black men, heartbreak carries an additional layer of complexity. Society often tells us that strength means silence, that real men don't cry, and that emotional vulnerability is a weakness. These messages trap us in a cycle of pain that we don't know how to break.

I wrote this book to start a conversation that is long overdue.

Purpose

The purpose of this book is simple but profound: to help Black men heal. To offer a voice to those who have been taught to suffer in silence. To provide tools, insights, and stories that can guide you through the pain of heartbreak and toward a place of wholeness and strength.

Heartbreak isn't just an individual experience—it's a communal one. When a Black man suffers silently, his family, friends, and community feel the ripple effects. By addressing our pain, we don't just heal ourselves; we create a blueprint for others to follow.

This book isn't just about heartbreak. It's about breaking cycles. It's about confronting the generational and cultural norms that have kept us from truly thriving. It's about redefining what it means to be strong, to be whole, and to be a man.

Personal Story and Context

In 2024, I faced heartbreak that changed everything. The relationship I thought would last forever ended abruptly, leaving me questioning everything I thought I knew about myself, love, and life. At first, I tried to do what I had always done: bury the pain, keep moving, and pretend I was fine. But the more I suppressed it, the more it consumed me.

By May of that year, the weight of my emotions pushed me to a breaking point. I found myself contemplating suicide, convinced that the silence I carried was too much to bear. I felt ashamed of my pain, trapped by the belief that no one would understand or care.

But in that darkest moment, something shifted. I realized that silence was not my savior—it was my oppressor. If I wanted to heal, I had to confront the pain, not hide from it. I had to acknowledge the stories and wounds I had carried for years, and I had to make the choice to live—not just for myself, but for the people who loved me and the future I still had the power to create.

Writing this book became part of my healing journey. It allowed me to process my own experiences while also recognizing the patterns I've seen in so many other Black men. As a QMHP, CSAC, and RPRS, I've worked with men who carry similar stories—of heartbreak, loss, and the silence that follows. This book is for them, and it's for you.

Addressing the Silence Black Men Face

Black men are often told to be strong, but strength is rarely defined in a way that allows us to feel human. We're expected to shoulder the weight of the world while hiding our emotions behind a mask of invincibility. This expectation is suffocating, and it's killing us.

Consider the statistics:

- Black men are significantly less likely to seek mental health treatment than their white counterparts (CDC, 2020).

- Nearly 64% of Black children grow up in single-parent households, often leaving boys without male role models who demonstrate emotional vulnerability (U.S. Census Bureau, 2020).

- Suicide rates among Black men have been steadily increasing, a stark reminder of the dangers of unaddressed pain (APA, 2021).

These numbers aren't just statistics—they're stories. Stories of men who felt they had no one to turn to. Stories of families grieving in silence because they didn't know how to break through the walls their loved ones had built.

This silence doesn't just harm us—it harms everyone around us. It creates distance in our relationships, stifles our potential, and perpetuates the cycle of unhealed trauma. But it doesn't have to be this way.

By breaking the silence, we can begin to heal. We can redefine what it means to be strong, to be whole, and to be free.

A Call to Action

This book is more than a guide—it's an invitation. An invitation to sit with your pain, to explore its roots, and to take the first steps toward healing. It's an invitation to rewrite your story, not just for yourself, but for the people who love you and the generations who will follow in your footsteps.

To every Black man who has ever felt unheard, unseen, or unloved: this is for you. You are not alone. Your pain is valid, and your healing is possible. Together, we can break the silence and create a new narrative—one of resilience, vulnerability, and hope.

Let's begin this journey.

Chapter 1: Understanding Heartbreak

Heartbreak is a universal experience. It strips us of certainty, stability, and connection, leaving behind a void that often feels impossible to fill. But for Black men, heartbreak carries unique complexities. It is not just about the loss of love; it is intertwined with layers of unspoken expectations, generational wounds, and societal pressures that demand strength at the expense of vulnerability.

This chapter isn't just about defining heartbreak—it's about confronting its weight. It's about peeling back the layers of emotional, physical, and mental pain to understand how heartbreak affects us and why it's so difficult to navigate. Most importantly, it's about acknowledging that we are not alone in our struggles.

Heartbreak has a way of coming for us when we least expect it, catching us off guard. The world continues to move around us, but internally, we're frozen. We know that the world expects us to keep moving, to keep going, but the truth is, sometimes we can't. Sometimes we need to stop and feel what we're feeling, even if that means confronting the mess of our emotions head-on.

The Emotional, Physical, and Mental Toll of Heartbreak

Heartbreak is often dismissed as something we should "just get over," but its impact is far deeper than most people realize. Studies have shown that emotional pain activates the same neural pathways as physical pain (National Institutes of Health, 2018). That's why heartbreak feels like a literal ache in your chest, a tightening in your throat, or an overwhelming heaviness in your body. The body feels it. The mind feels it. There's a physical manifestation to our emotional suffering that we often try to ignore.

For Black men, this pain is often compounded by silence. Society doesn't give us permission to grieve openly. We're told to "man up," to "keep it moving," and to hide our emotions behind a façade of toughness.

This creates a dangerous cycle:

Emotionally, we suppress our feelings, disconnecting from ourselves and those around us.

Physically, the stress of unprocessed emotions manifests as headaches, fatigue, or even heart problems.

Mentally, we spiral into self-doubt, depression, or anxiety, feeling as though we've failed not only ourselves but also the people who depend on us.

We've been taught that being a Black man means shouldering everything—our burdens, our fears, and our grief—in silence. Our emotional pain is often disregarded or brushed off because there's this belief that we don't have the luxury of feeling vulnerable. But the truth is, vulnerability is not a weakness. It's our strength. It's what makes us human.

Personal Insight: I remember the weeks following my breakup in 2024. Every morning felt like a battle to get out of bed. My chest felt heavy, my thoughts raced with questions I couldn't answer, and my body felt as though it was carrying twice its normal weight. I told myself I was fine, but my sleepless nights and lack of appetite told a different story. It wasn't just the end of a relationship—it was the unravelling of the identity I had built around it. My mental health deteriorated, and addiction destroyed what was left of any normalcy.

The hardest part about heartbreak is that you can feel as if you're drowning. On the outside, no one would know. You continue to show up, go through the motions, and pretend everything is fine. But inside, there's a storm. You try to make sense of it, but you can't. You feel as if the very foundation you've built for yourself is collapsing, and you wonder if you'll ever find your way out.

The Layers of Heartbreak

Heartbreak is rarely just about the person we lose. It's about what their absence reveals—the wounds, fears, and insecurities we've carried long before they entered our lives. For Black men, these layers often run deeper, shaped by the generational and societal forces that define our experiences.

The Surface Wound

The most obvious layer of heartbreak is the immediate pain of loss: the breakup, the betrayal, or the realization that the relationship we cherished has come to an end. This pain is raw and visceral, and it's often the first thing we focus on. But beneath this layer lies much more.

The deeper layers of heartbreak aren't always easy to see at first. We are often consumed by the pain of the immediate loss—the nights spent awake, the sadness, the regrets. But with time, we realize that the pain is more than just about the relationship ending. It's about what it represented. That relationship might have been our anchor, our safe place, our sense of belonging. Its loss brings up so much more than the ending of something external—it brings up feelings of abandonment, feelings of failure, and the fear that we'll never find our way back to peace.

The Unspoken Fears

Heartbreak taps into our deepest insecurities—fears of being unworthy, of never being enough, of being abandoned. These fears are often rooted in childhood experiences or past relationships that left scars we never fully addressed.

Example Insight: One client I worked with struggled to move on after his wife left him. Through our conversations, he realized that his heartbreak wasn't just about losing his partner—it was about reliving the abandonment he felt as a child when his father walked out.

Our fears are complex. They don't always surface in ways we recognize immediately. Sometimes, heartbreak pulls back the curtain on fears we've long tried to hide, fears that we are unworthy of love, that we are destined to fail, or that the very thing we need most—connection— is out of reach. These are the shadows we must face if we're to heal.

The Generational Wounds

Many Black men carry the weight of generational trauma—unresolved pain passed down through families. Maybe it's the silence of fathers who never expressed emotion, the struggles of mothers who bore the burden of single parenthood, or the societal pressures that taught us to value survival over emotional well-being. Heartbreak often reopens these wounds, forcing us to confront not just the pain of the present, but the legacies of the past.

There's a long history of Black men being taught to suppress their emotions, to "be strong," to carry the weight of their family and community on their backs without asking for help or showing vulnerability. This pressure comes from society, but it is also deeply ingrained in family systems. In our culture, many of us were raised in environments where emotions weren't openly discussed. Crying was discouraged. Feeling was seen as a sign of weakness.

Personal Insight: For me, heartbreak wasn't just about losing a partner—it was about realizing how much of my self-worth I had tied to someone else. Growing up in a two-parent household, I still often felt the absence of my father who worked two jobs for my entire upbringing. When my relationship ended, it brought those feelings to the surface, leaving me to wrestle with questions I hadn't dared to ask before: Am I worthy of love? Can I trust someone not to leave?

The Role of Silence

Silence is one of the most common ways Black men cope with heartbreak. We retreat, withdrawing into ourselves because we've been taught that vulnerability is a sign of weakness. But silence isn't healing—it's hiding.

When we bottle up our emotions, they don't disappear. Instead, they manifest in other ways:

Anger that lashes out at the people closest to us.

Numbness that makes it impossible to connect with others.

Self-destructive behaviors, like substance abuse or risky decisions, as a way to escape the pain.

Silence, though often seen as a means of control, is not the solution. It only breeds isolation and prolongs the suffering. To heal, we must break the silence. We must be willing to speak our truth, even when it's painful.

Cultural Insight: In many Black families, vulnerability is rarely modeled. We're often raised with phrases like "stop crying" or "get over it," creating an environment where emotional expression feels unsafe. This silence is a learned behavior, passed down through generations, but it's a cycle we have the power to break.

We must redefine what it means to be strong. Strength isn't about bottling up our emotions; it's about acknowledging them, allowing ourselves to feel, and then using that understanding to move forward.

Personal Experiences with Depression and Trauma

Heartbreak doesn't just hurt—it can lead to depression and trauma that linger long after the relationship ends. For me, the pain of my breakup in 2024 pushed me to the brink. By May, I found myself contemplating suicide, convinced that the weight of my emotions was too much to bear.

Depression doesn't announce itself loudly—it creeps in quietly. It's the loss of interest in things you used to love, the feeling of being trapped in your own mind, the voice that tells you that your pain doesn't matter.

But here's what I've learned: depression lies. It tells you that you're alone when you're not. It tells you that healing isn't possible when it is.

Professional Insight: As a QMHP, I've worked with clients who believed their depression was a personal failing rather than a natural response to trauma. Helping them reframe their pain—not as weakness, but as a signal that something needed attention—was often the first step toward healing.

Action Step: If you're struggling with depression, don't wait to seek help. Reach out to a therapist, a trusted friend, or a crisis hotline. Your pain is real, but so is your ability to heal.

A Call to Acknowledge

Understanding heartbreak means confronting it in all its complexity. It's not just about what happened—it's about what it reveals. It's about sitting with the pain, peeling back its layers, and giving yourself permission to feel, to grieve, and to grow.

This chapter has laid the foundation for understanding heartbreak

as more than just a moment of loss. In the next chapter, we'll explore how to begin the healing process—starting with the courage to face your pain and take the first steps forward.

Closing Thoughts for Chapter 1

Heartbreak isn't just an ending—it's a beginning. It's an opportunity to uncover the stories you've been telling yourself and to rewrite them in a way that empowers you. Remember, you are not defined by the pain you've experienced, but by how you choose to rise from it.

Chapter 2: Steps Toward Healing

Healing is often spoken of as if it's a destination—a place we arrive at when we've finally "gotten over it." But the truth is, healing is not a destination. It's a journey, one that requires patience, courage, and a willingness to confront the parts of ourselves we'd rather avoid. It's a process that unfolds over time, requiring us to revisit our pain, not to relive it, but to learn from it, release it, and grow. It's easy to wish for a quick fix, to want the pain to disappear, but real healing can't be rushed. It can't be forced. It requires that we walk through the pain, face it, and allow it to shape us in ways that ultimately make us stronger.

For Black men, this journey is often made more complicated by societal expectations that tell us to move on quickly, to toughen up, to mask our pain. From a young age, we're taught that showing vulnerability is a sign of weakness. In many ways, we are forced to live up to this image of strength—strength that is often misinterpreted as silence, as stoicism, as the inability to acknowledge our hurt. But real healing can't happen in the absence of truth. We need to be willing to look at ourselves, to confront the rawness of our emotions, and to ask for help when we need it. Just as a physical injury needs care and attention, so too does emotional pain.

This chapter is about taking the first steps toward healing. It's about acknowledging your pain, finding the support you need, and building routines that help you trust yourself again. Healing isn't easy, but it's worth it—and it's possible. With the right mindset, support, and tools, you can move beyond the hurt and into a place of peace.

Acknowledging the Pain

The first and most important step in healing is acknowledging the pain. This sounds simple, but for many of us, it's the hardest part. We've been conditioned to believe that admitting we're hurt makes us weak, that it's better to push through the pain than to sit with it. But ignoring the pain doesn't make it go away—it only makes it harder to heal. Just as you wouldn't ignore a physical injury, you can't ignore the wounds of the heart. The more you suppress your feelings, the more they fester beneath the surface, until one day, they'll come out in ways you can't control.

Acknowledging your pain means giving yourself permission to feel it fully. It means saying, "I'm not okay right now, and that's okay." This isn't about wallowing or staying stuck in your hurt. It's about giving yourself the space to recognize that you are human, and that feeling pain is part of the human experience. You don't have to be ashamed of your hurt. You don't have to hide it to meet someone else's standards of strength. True strength lies in vulnerability—the courage to admit that you are hurting and that it's okay to take the time to heal.

Personal Insight: After my breakup, I spent weeks pretending everything was fine. I threw myself into work, avoided my friends, and told myself I just needed to "move on." But the more I ignored my pain, the heavier it became. It wasn't until I sat down one night and let myself cry—really cry—that I began to feel even a glimmer of relief. That moment of acknowledgment wasn't the end of my pain, but it was the beginning of my healing. It was the first time I allowed myself to confront the reality of what I was feeling, to say, "This hurts, and it's okay to hurt."

Reflection Prompt: Take a moment to write down what you're feeling right now. Be honest with yourself. Are you angry? Sad? Confused? There's no right or wrong answer—just let the words flow. Give yourself permission to feel the full spectrum of your emotions without judgment. What you write doesn't have to make sense immediately. Just let the emotions out. This is the first step toward releasing them.

The Importance of Naming Emotions

When we don't acknowledge our pain, it often shows up in other ways—anger, frustration, or numbness. We may find ourselves lashing out at loved ones or retreating inward, unable to connect with anyone, even those who care for us. Naming your emotions is a powerful way to take control of your healing process. It allows you to understand what you're feeling and why, which is the first step toward moving through it. The more specific you can be with your emotions, the clearer the path to healing becomes. Often, we try to push emotions like sadness or anger aside because we don't understand them. But if we can start to name them, we can begin to untangle the mess inside.

Practical Exercise: Try using a feelings wheel (available online) to identify specific emotions you're experiencing. For example, instead of saying, "I feel bad," you might say, "I feel betrayed," or "I feel overwhelmed." This specificity helps you better understand your pain. Naming the emotion is like giving it a shape, a form that you can confront instead of letting it stay a vague, all-encompassing feeling of "badness." The more clearly you can name your emotions, the better you can address them.

Finding Support and Embracing Therapy

Healing doesn't happen in isolation. While it's natural to want to retreat after heartbreak, finding support is crucial. Whether it's a trusted friend, a family member, or a professional therapist, having someone to talk to can make all the difference. We all need a safe space to share our pain, to speak our truths, and to be heard without judgment. Connection is a key part of healing, and sometimes that connection comes in the form of other people—people who can help us bear our burdens, people who can help us see beyond our pain.

The Power of Connection: Studies have shown that social support is one of the most significant factors in emotional recovery (American Psychological Association, 2021). Sharing your pain with someone who listens without judgment can lighten the burden you're carrying. There's immense power in speaking your truth to another person who understands—someone who doesn't try to fix your pain but simply acknowledges it, sits with it alongside you.

Personal Insight: I'll never forget the first time I opened up to a friend about my heartbreak. I expected him to tell me to "man up" or dismiss my feelings, but instead, he listened. He didn't try to fix anything—he just let me talk. That conversation reminded me that I wasn't alone, and it gave me the courage to seek professional help. It was the first time I truly realized that I didn't have to carry my pain alone.

Embracing Therapy

For many Black men, the idea of therapy feels foreign—or even unnecessary. We've been taught to solve our problems on our own, to rely on our strength and willpower. But therapy isn't about weakness—it's about growth. It's about giving yourself the tools to understand your pain and move forward. It's an opportunity to gain new perspectives and find healthy ways to cope with the emotional pain that we often carry for far too long. Therapy is not an admission of failure—it's a step toward taking control of your emotional health.

What Therapy Offers:

A safe space to explore your emotions without fear of judgment.

Strategies for coping with pain, stress, and anxiety.

A chance to break unhealthy patterns and build healthier ones.

Practical Advice: If therapy feels intimidating, start small. Look for therapists who specialize in working with men of color or consider online platforms like Therapy for Black Men or Black Men Heal. Many offer free or low-cost sessions to make therapy more accessible. Therapy is not a one-time fix; it's an ongoing process that supports long-term healing. If the idea of traditional therapy feels overwhelming, try online counseling services where you can access help in a way that feels more comfortable for you.

Building Healing Routines and Self-Trust

Healing isn't just about what you feel—it's about what you do. Creating routines that support your mental, emotional, and physical well-being can help you regain a sense of control and stability. Sometimes, the pain can make us feel lost, unsure of where to turn. Building routines can help guide us, giving us structure and stability while we work through our emotions. It's not about perfection; it's about consistency. It's about taking one step at a time, each day, until you feel more like yourself again.

Journaling

Writing down your thoughts and emotions is one of the most effective ways to process pain. Journaling allows you to get the chaos out of your head and onto paper, where it feels more manageable. Putting your emotions into words helps externalize them, making them easier to understand and ultimately release.

Practical Exercise: Each morning, spend five minutes writing about how you feel. Don't worry about grammar or structure—just let the words flow. Over time, you'll start to see patterns that can help you understand your pain better. Journaling is a powerful tool for self-reflection, and it helps bring clarity in times of confusion.

Movement and Exercise

Physical activity isn't just good for your body—it's good for your mind. Exercise releases endorphins, which can improve your mood and reduce stress. But the benefits of exercise go beyond just feeling better physically—it's a way of showing yourself that you're capable of taking control of your body and your emotions. Physical movement is an act of self-care and self-respect.

Personal Insight: For me, going to the gym became a lifeline after my breakup. It wasn't just about staying in shape—it was about proving to myself that I was still capable of growth. Each time I lifted a heavier weight or ran a little farther, I felt a sense of accomplishment that reminded me I was stronger than my pain

.

Practical Advice: Start small. Even a 10-minute walk can make a difference. Find an activity you enjoy, whether it's yoga, dancing, or playing basketball, and make it part of your routine. You don't have to become a fitness expert overnight. The goal is to move your body, to feel alive, and to remind yourself that you're still in control.

Setting Small Goals

Heartbreak can leave you feeling aimless, but setting small, achievable goals can help you rebuild confidence. When you feel lost, accomplishing small tasks can give you a sense of purpose and remind you of what you're capable of.

Practical Exercise: Write down one goal you'd like to accomplish this week. It could be as simple as cooking a healthy meal or calling a friend. Celebrate your success when you achieve it. These small wins are victories in the healing process.

Rebuilding Trust in Yourself

Heartbreak often shakes our confidence, making us question our worth and our ability to make good decisions. Rebuilding trust in yourself is a gradual process, but it starts with small acts of self-care and self-respect. Every time you take action to care for yourself, you are reinforcing the belief that you deserve love, respect, and kindness.

Action Step: Identify one way you can show yourself kindness today. Maybe it's taking a break when you're overwhelmed or saying no to something that doesn't serve you. These small acts add up over time, reminding you that you're worthy of care and compassion.

Closing Thoughts for Chapter 2

Healing isn't a straight line—it's a journey with ups and downs, steps forward and steps back. But each step you take—acknowledging your pain, finding support, building routines—is a step closer to the person you're meant to become. You have the strength within you to heal, to grow, and to rise again. In the next chapter, we'll explore how to rebuild your confidence and purpose, rediscovering who you are and what you're capable of after heartbreak.

Chapter 3: Rebuilding Confidence and Purpose

Heartbreak has a way of shaking us to our core. It leaves us questioning who we are, what we're worth, and where we're headed. For many of us, it's not just the loss of a relationship—it's the loss of the identity and dreams we tied to that relationship. Our sense of self can feel shattered, as if the foundation that supported everything we believed about ourselves is gone. The loss can be so profound that we feel as if we've lost our way. In these moments, it's easy to lose sight of who we are without that person, that connection, and the future we envisioned together. But as painful as heartbreak is, it also offers an unexpected opportunity. It's an invitation to reconnect with yourself, to rediscover your purpose, and to rebuild your confidence—one step at a time. This chapter is about taking those steps, even when it feels overwhelming, to rebuild your sense of self and purpose after the devastation of heartbreak.

Reconnecting with Yourself

After heartbreak, it's easy to feel lost, as if the version of yourself you knew is gone. When a relationship ends, it often takes with it pieces of your identity that were intertwined with that connection. The person you were as a partner, the dreams you shared, and the goals you pursued as a unit can all feel like they've evaporated overnight. The person who you were in the relationship with might seem like a stranger, and the future you once envisioned can feel unreachable.

But rebuilding confidence starts with reconnecting with who you are outside of the relationship. What are your values? What brings you joy? What makes you feel alive? These are the questions that allow you to rediscover yourself, to peel back the layers of who you were and who you can become.

Personal Insight: After my breakup, I realized how much of my identity I had tied to being someone's partner. I spent so much time trying to make the relationship work that I lost sight of who I was outside of it. My passions, my goals, and even my self-worth had become entangled with the relationship. Reconnecting with myself meant rediscovering those things I had neglected, like journaling, exercising, and mentoring young men in my community. These activities were more than just hobbies; they were expressions of who I was at my core.

Practical Exercise: Take out a piece of paper and write down five things you loved about yourself before the relationship. These could be hobbies, traits, or achievements—anything that made you feel proud and connected to who you are. Then, write down one way you can bring each of those things back into your life. Maybe it's picking up that hobby again or starting a new project that aligns with your values. This process will help you rediscover the person you were before the relationship, and remind you that you are still that person, even after the heartbreak.

Letting Go of External Validation

One of the hardest parts of heartbreak is learning to stop seeking validation from others. For many of us, relationships become a source of self-worth. We feel valued and seen through the eyes of our partner, and when that relationship ends, we often feel unworthy or unlovable. We may believe that our value is determined by someone else's perception of us. This external validation can leave us feeling like we're not enough when the relationship is over.

But healing means learning to validate ourselves from within. We need to rediscover our intrinsic worth, separate from any external source. This process involves accepting ourselves for who we are, without needing someone else's approval to feel good about who we are.

Reflection Prompt: Think about a time when you felt proud of yourself, independent of anyone else's opinion. What were you doing? How can you recreate that feeling in your life now? This is a great way to tap into the internal sense of fulfillment that doesn't rely on the approval or love of others.

Practical Advice: Start small. Set aside time each day to do something just for yourself, whether it's cooking a meal you love, listening to your favorite music, or spending time in nature. These moments are a reminder that your happiness doesn't depend on someone else; it's something you can create for yourself.

Setting Achievable Goals and Rediscovering Purpose

Heartbreak can disrupt your sense of purpose. When your future seems so tied to someone else, it's natural to feel directionless when the relationship ends. Goals and purpose give your life structure and meaning, and without them, it can feel like you're drifting. Rebuilding confidence after heartbreak requires setting small, achievable goals that will help you regain momentum and rediscover the purpose that was lost in the aftermath.

Start Small, Dream Big

Confidence isn't rebuilt overnight—it's earned through small wins. Start with goals that feel manageable, things you can do even when you're feeling low. These small goals provide the structure to rebuild your life piece by piece. As you accomplish these smaller tasks, you'll gradually gain the confidence to tackle bigger ones.

Personal Insight: After my breakup, my first goal was simply to get out of bed at a consistent time each morning. It seemed trivial, but it gave me a sense of control over my day. From there, I set bigger goals—completing a certification program, reconnecting with old friends, and eventually writing this book. Each goal, no matter how small, reinforced the idea that I was still capable of growth, that I could still make progress even in the midst of pain.

Practical Exercise: Write down one goal for this week, one for this month, and one for the next six months. Make sure each goal is specific and measurable. For example:

This week: Go for a 15-minute walk every day.

This month: Read one book on personal growth.

Six months: Enroll in a class or pursue a passion project.

Each of these goals, though small in the grand scheme of things, will contribute to your healing and help you regain a sense of control and direction. Celebrate the small victories along the way and recognize that they add up to bigger progress over time.

Rediscovering Your Purpose

Purpose is what gives our lives meaning, and after heartbreak, it's easy to lose sight of it. The void left by the end of a relationship can feel like it stretches endlessly. But heartbreak can also be a catalyst—a chance to reevaluate what matters most to you and align your life with those values. It's an opportunity to reframe your goals, discover new passions, and find a purpose that is independent of someone else.

Reflection Prompt: Think about a time when you felt truly fulfilled. What were you doing? Who were you with? How can you bring those elements back into your life? This reflection helps uncover the deeper meaning behind the activities and experiences that make you feel alive. It's a chance to reconnect with your deeper purpose.

Professional Insight: In my work as a QMHP, I've seen how rediscovering purpose can transform lives. One client, after losing a long-term partner, found renewed meaning by volunteering at a local shelter—a passion he had neglected for years. For him, helping others became a way to heal his own heart. Finding a cause greater than himself not only filled the void left by the breakup but also gave him a sense of fulfillment that carried him through the hardest moments.

Surrounding Yourself with Positivity

The people you surround yourself with have a profound impact on your confidence and mindset. Rebuilding confidence often means reevaluating your relationships and seeking out connections that uplift and inspire you. Negative or toxic relationships can drag you down, while positive ones provide encouragement and accountability.

Identifying Toxic Patterns

Not all relationships are healthy, and heartbreak can sometimes reveal the people who were more draining than supportive. It's important to identify these toxic patterns and take the necessary steps to protect your emotional well-being. Rebuilding confidence may require setting boundaries or stepping away from relationships that no longer serve you.

Reflection Prompt: Think about the people in your life. Who makes you feel supported, understood, and valued? Who drains your energy or adds to your stress? It's important to distinguish between relationships that build you up and those that bring you down.

Practical Advice: Write down three qualities you value in a relationship (e.g., honesty, support, mutual respect). Use these qualities as a guide when deciding which relationships to nurture and which to step back from. Surrounding yourself with people who support your growth can accelerate your healing process.

Building a Supportive Circle

Healing is easier when you have people cheering you on. Seek out friends, mentors, or even online communities that encourage your growth and remind you of your worth. The connections you cultivate during this time can make all the difference in your ability to rebuild confidence.

Personal Insight: After my breakup, I found strength in my community. Whether it was a conversation with a mentor or a group workout with friends, these connections reminded me that I wasn't alone—and that I had people who believed in me, even when I struggled to believe in myself. The support of those around me helped me to keep moving forward, even when the road felt impossible.

Action Step: Reach out to one person who inspires or supports you. It could be as simple as sending a text or scheduling a coffee chat. Let them know how much their support means to you. Strengthening these connections is a vital part of rebuilding confidence.

Fostering Self-Positivity

Surrounding yourself with positivity isn't just about other people—it's also about how you talk to yourself. Negative self-talk can erode your confidence, while affirmations and self-compassion can help you rebuild it. The way you speak to yourself during this time matters. Self-kindness and positive self-talk are crucial tools in rebuilding a sense of self-worth and confidence.

Practical Exercise: Every morning, write down one affirmation about yourself. For example: "I am resilient," or "I am capable of growth." Repeat it to yourself throughout the day. This simple practice can help counter

act the negative thoughts that arise during times of hardship and create a foundation for positive self-belief.

Closing Thoughts for Chapter 3

Rebuilding confidence and purpose isn't about erasing the past—it's about learning from it and using it to create a brighter future. Every small step you take—whether it's reconnecting with yourself, setting a goal, or reaching out to someone who inspires you—is a step toward the life you deserve. By rebuilding your confidence, rediscovering your purpose, and surrounding yourself with positivity, you create a life that is rooted in your own strength and authenticity.

Chapter 4: Healing Relationships

Heartbreak doesn't just affect the person going through it—it ripples outward, touching the lives of family, friends, and loved ones. When we're in pain, it's natural to withdraw, retreating into ourselves to protect our pride or shield others from our struggles. Yet isolation comes at a cost, not just to us but to the relationships that matter most. We think we're protecting our loved ones from our hurt by pulling away, but in reality, we're unintentionally creating distance that deepens the pain.

Healing isn't just about mending your own heart—it's about repairing the bonds that heartbreak may have strained. Relationships require attention and care, especially during difficult times. The emotional wounds we carry from heartbreak don't just affect us—they impact the people who love us. How we engage with those around us during these challenging times can either fortify or weaken those relationships. This chapter explores the ripple effect of isolation, offers strategies for rebuilding trust, and highlights the importance of setting healthy boundaries and cultivating connections that foster growth.

The Ripple Effect of Isolation

Isolation often feels like the safest response to heartbreak. We tell ourselves that pulling away will protect us from further pain or that our emotions are too much for others to handle. But the truth is, the more we isolate, the more disconnected we become—not just from others, but from ourselves. Isolation is a cycle that makes us feel safer, but in reality, it only reinforces feelings of loneliness and alienation. We may feel that our hurt is too much for others to bear, so we shut ourselves off, convinced that no one can understand what we're going through.

Research has consistently shown the dangers of prolonged isolation. It increases the risk of depression, anxiety, and even physical health issues such as high blood pressure and weakened immunity (Holt-Lunstad, 2017). For Black men, isolation is often compounded by societal pressures that discourage vulnerability. We're taught to handle struggles in silence, which makes it even harder to reach out when we need support the most. This silence becomes a barrier to connection, leaving us to carry our pain alone, without the comfort of shared understanding or emotional relief.

Cultural Insight: Many Black families operate under unspoken rules that discourage discussing emotional pain. Phrases like "what happens in this house stays in this house" create a culture of silence that makes it difficult for men to express vulnerability. This silence, passed down through generations, leaves many Black men feeling isolated even in the presence of loved ones (Minority Health, 2022). It's a pattern that makes it hard to ask for support, even when we desperately need it. Over time, this silence can create a deep divide between us and those who care for us, as they may feel locked out, unsure of how to offer help or understanding.

Personal Insight: I remember how my own isolation after my breakup affected those closest to me. My family and friends remained worried, felt shut out, and my colleagues sensed something was wrong but didn't know how to approach me. At the time, I thought pulling away was the best way to protect everyone, but in hindsight, I realized how much damage that isolation caused to the people who cared about me. I had convinced myself that I was sparing them from my pain, but instead, I alienated them, further deepening my loneliness.

Recognizing the Signs of Harmful Isolation

Sometimes, isolation becomes so familiar that we don't even realize the impact it's having on our lives. Here are a few signs to watch for:

You avoid calls or messages from loved ones, preferring the quiet of being alone.

Social events or gatherings feel overwhelming or pointless, leaving you retreating into solitude.

You feel like no one will understand your pain, so you stop trying to explain or share.

You find comfort in the predictability of being alone, even if it leaves you feeling empty or restless.

A key part of healing is recognizing these patterns and acknowledging that isolation isn't providing the relief we imagine it does. It's simply prolonging the pain. Opening up to others, even when it feels impossible, is the first step toward reconnecting and healing.

Reflection Prompt: Think about a time when you isolated yourself from others. How did it affect your relationships? What would you do differently now? Acknowledging the damage caused by isolation is an important part of the healing process.

Rebuilding Trust with Family and Friends

Heartbreak can create distance in even the closest relationships, but trust can be rebuilt. The foundation of trust is vulnerability—allowing others to see the real you, even when you feel raw or broken. Being vulnerable isn't a sign of weakness; it's an expression of courage and strength. When we open up and allow others to witness our pain, we create space for healing, not only for ourselves but also for the relationships that have been impacted by our withdrawal.

Start with Accountability

Rebuilding trust starts with taking accountability for your role in the disconnection. This doesn't mean blaming yourself for everything, but acknowledging where your actions—such as withdrawing or shutting people out—may have hurt others. Accountability is about recognizing that healing requires effort, not just from ourselves but from the relationships we cherish.

Practical Advice: When approaching a conversation to rebuild trust, focus on "I" statements. For example:

"I know I've been distant, and I want to apologize. I've been going through a lot, but I value our relationship and want to reconnect."

Acknowledging your own role in the disconnection allows the other person to feel heard and validated. It also creates a foundation for rebuilding trust, as it shows that you are willing to be open and honest about your feelings and actions.

Be Prepared for Reactions

Sometimes, the people you reconnect with might express hurt or frustration over your withdrawal. Be patient and willing to listen without becoming defensive. Their feelings are valid, just as yours are. Trust is rebuilt not just by speaking your truth, but by listening to others' truths as well. Rebuilding trust means allowing both parties to express their emotions without judgment or defensiveness.

Example Insight: I worked with a client who wanted to repair his relationship with his sister after months of silence following his divorce. During their first conversation, she expressed anger over feeling abandoned. Instead of shutting down, he listened and apologized, which allowed them to move forward with honesty and mutual understanding.

Action Step: Choose one person in your life you've grown distant from and initiate a conversation to rebuild trust. Make it a priority to listen to their feelings and share your own with openness and vulnerability. This isn't just about fixing the relationship—it's about learning to reconnect in ways that honor both parties.

Setting Healthy Boundaries

While reconnecting with loved ones is essential, setting boundaries is equally important. Boundaries protect your emotional health by ensuring that your needs are respected while maintaining the integrity of your relationships. Boundaries are not about shutting people out—they're about creating space for yourself and protecting your mental and emotional well-being.

What Healthy Boundaries Look Like

Boundaries aren't walls. They are clear lines that define what you need to feel safe, supported, and respected in your relationships. For example:

Limiting how much time you spend discussing painful topics. Sometimes, it's important to take a break from the intensity of grief and allow space for lighter, more positive conversations.

Asking for space when you need it, without cutting people off entirely. It's important to communicate when you need a moment to recharge without making others feel abandoned or rejected.

Communicating clearly when someone's behavior crosses a line. Boundaries mean knowing where your limits are and being able to enforce them in a way that maintains mutual respect.

Overcoming Guilt About Boundaries

Many people, especially those from collectivist cultures, struggle with guilt when setting boundaries. We're taught to prioritize others' needs over our own, which can make it feel selfish to say no. But boundaries are an act of self-respect, not selfishness. They allow you to show up as your best self, without compromising your emotional health.

Practical Advice: If you struggle with guilt, remind yourself that setting boundaries allows you to show up more fully in your relationships. When you're not overextended, you can give your best self to others.

Reflection Prompt: Think about a situation where you felt drained or overwhelmed because you didn't set a boundary. What could you do differently next time? Setting boundaries isn't about pushing people away—it's about ensuring that you can be present without losing yourself in the process.

Cultivating Supportive Connections

Healing is a journey that's easier when shared. Surrounding yourself with positive, supportive people can help you rebuild your confidence and remind you of your worth. Connections that are built on mutual respect, understanding, and shared growth are the relationships that will help you thrive.

Identify Who Lifts You Up

Take time to evaluate your relationships. Who makes you feel seen, valued, and supported? These are the people who deserve your time and energy. Focus on nurturing those connections while letting go of relationships that drain your energy or add unnecessary stress.

Personal Insight: After my breakup, I made the mistake of leaning on a friend who often dismissed my feelings as "dramatic." It wasn't until I started spending time with people who truly listened and supported me that I began to heal. True support isn't about being told what we want to hear—it's about being heard, validated, and encouraged to grow.

Create New Connections

Sometimes, heartbreak provides an opportunity to build new relationships. Joining support groups, attending community events, or even starting a new hobby can introduce you to people who share your values and interests. New connections allow you to expand your support network, building a community that enhances your healing journey.

Cultural Insight: Historically, Black communities have thrived on collective resilience, from church congregations to neighborhood networks. Reconnecting with a community, whether through volunteering, activism, or creative pursuits, can provide a sense of purpose and belonging

National Institutes of Health, 2018). These connections can offer the support you need, while also allowing you to give back and create positive change in your own life and the lives of others.

Fostering Positivity in Your Space

Surrounding yourself with positivity isn't just about the people in your life—it's about the energy you allow into your space. Take stock of the media you consume, the conversations you engage in, and the environments you spend time in. Your physical and mental spaces should nurture your growth, not hinder it.

Action Step: Spend one week curating a positive environment. Replace negative media with uplifting books or podcasts, limit time spent with people who drain you, and seek out spaces that inspire peace and joy. This positive shift in your environment can help promote healing by surrounding yourself with energy that uplifts you.

Closing Thoughts for Chapter 4

Healing relationships after heartbreak is not about returning to what was—it's about creating something stronger. By addressing the ripple effect of isolation, rebuilding trust, setting boundaries, and cultivating connections, you're not just healing yourself—you're creating a foundation for healthier, more fulfilling relationships. Healing isn't a solitary process, and the relationships you nurture along the way will help you grow in ways you never imagined. Through vulnerability, accountability, and respect, you can rebuild not only your heart but the relationships that truly matter.

Chapter 5: Breaking Generational Cycles of Pain

Generational cycles are powerful. They shape the way we see the world, how we process emotions, and how we interact with others. For Black men, these cycles often carry the weight of systemic oppression, fractured family structures, and unspoken traumas passed down through generations.

Breaking these cycles isn't just an act of personal healing—it's an act of liberation. It's about honoring where we come from while choosing to create a new path forward. This chapter explores what it means to recognize and break generational cycles, offering tools for forgiveness, self-compassion, and building habits that inspire change for future generations.

Understanding Generational Trauma

Generational trauma refers to the emotional wounds passed down from one generation to the next. These wounds are not just personal—they're cultural, historical, and systemic. For Black families, the legacy of slavery, segregation, and systemic racism continues to influence how we navigate relationships, emotions, and survival.

The Science of Inherited Trauma

Research shows that trauma can be passed down biologically through changes in gene expression, a phenomenon known as epigenetics (National Institutes of Health, 2018). This means that the emotional and physical stress experienced by one generation can affect the DNA of the next, influencing how we respond to stress, fear, and attachment.

- **Example Insight:** A 2015 study found that descendants of Holocaust survivors showed higher levels of stress hormones, even decades after the trauma occurred. Similarly, Black Americans continue to experience the psychological impact of historical oppression, affecting how families communicate, cope, and connect (American Psychological Association, 2021).
- **Reflection Prompt:** Think about the emotional patterns in your family. Are there behaviors, fears, or beliefs that seem to repeat across generations?

How Generational Trauma Shows Up

Generational trauma often manifests in subtle but powerful ways:

- **Emotional Suppression:** A reluctance to express vulnerability, stemming from the need to appear strong in the face of adversity.
- **Conflict Avoidance:** A tendency to avoid confrontation, rooted in fear of further harm or rejection.
- **Codependency:** Prioritizing the needs of others over your own, often modeled by caregivers who sacrificed their well-being to protect their families.

Understanding these patterns is the first step toward breaking them.

Recognizing Cycles in Your Life

Generational cycles are often so ingrained that we don't realize we're repeating them. Recognizing these cycles requires self-awareness and a willingness to look critically at the behaviors, beliefs, and dynamics we've inherited.

Identifying Patterns

Start by reflecting on the dynamics in your family:

- How did your parents or caregivers express love?
- Were emotions openly discussed or avoided?
- What beliefs about masculinity, vulnerability, or success were instilled in you?
- **Personal Insight:** Growing up, I rarely saw my father express emotion. He believed that being stoic was the only way to survive in a world that often-dehumanized Black men. While his intentions were protective, they left me struggling to express my own emotions as an adult. It wasn't until I recognized this pattern that I could begin to change it.

Breaking the Cycle

Breaking generational cycles doesn't mean rejecting your family—it means choosing to evolve. It's about acknowledging the pain that was passed down while deciding to create a new legacy for yourself and those who follow.

- **Practical Exercise:** Write a letter to one of your caregivers, describing the patterns you've noticed and how they've affected you. This isn't about blame—it's about clarity and understanding.

The Role of Forgiveness and Self-Compassion

Forgiveness is a cornerstone of breaking generational cycles. It's not about condoning harmful behavior but about releasing the hold it has on you.

Forgiving Your Family

Forgiving family members doesn't mean excusing their actions—it means recognizing that they, too, were shaped by their own traumas. Many of our parents and grandparents did the best they could with the tools they had, even if those tools were inadequate.

- **Reflection Prompt:** Think about one family member whose actions have hurt you. What might they have been carrying that influenced their behavior?

- **Personal Insight:** Forgiving my father for his emotional distance was one of the hardest things I've ever done. But when I considered the pressures he faced as a Black man in a hostile world, I realized that his silence wasn't about me—it was his way of surviving.

Practicing Self-Compassion

Self-compassion is equally important. Breaking cycles is hard work, and it's natural to stumble along the way. Being kind to yourself means recognizing your progress, even when it feels small.

- **Practical Exercise:** Each evening, write down one thing you did that day to break a cycle—whether it's setting a boundary, expressing an emotion, or choosing self-care. Celebrate these victories, no matter how minor they seem.

Building New Habits for Future Generations

Breaking cycles isn't just about healing yourself—it's about creating a foundation for healthier relationships and emotional habits that can be passed down to the next generation.

Developing Emotional Intelligence

Emotional intelligence is the ability to recognize, understand, and manage your emotions. It's a skill that can transform how you interact with others and how you model healthy behavior for future generations.

- **Practical Advice:** Practice naming your emotions regularly. For example, instead of saying, "I feel bad," try, "I feel disappointed because I expected a different outcome." This specificity helps you process emotions more effectively.

Setting Boundaries as a Legacy

Teaching children or younger relatives the importance of boundaries can break cycles of codependency and emotional exhaustion. When they see you prioritizing your well-being, they learn to do the same.

- **Example Insight:** I began teaching my nephew the power of saying no by modeling it in my own life. When he saw me set boundaries with work and friendships, it gave him permission to do the same in school and with his peers.

Fostering Connection Through Vulnerability

Vulnerability is a powerful way to break cycles of emotional suppression. Sharing your struggles and growth openly encourages others to do the same.

- **Cultural Insight:** In many African traditions, storytelling is a way to pass down wisdom and build connection. By sharing your story of breaking cycles, you contribute to a legacy of resilience and growth (National Institutes of Health, 2018).

Closing Thoughts for Chapter 5

Breaking generational cycles isn't just about healing yourself—it's about creating a ripple effect that transforms your relationships, your family, and your community. Each step you take—whether it's recognizing a pattern, forgiving a family member, or building a new habit—brings you closer to freedom.

In the next chapter, we'll explore how to thrive beyond heartbreak, building a life filled with joy, purpose, and connection.

Chapter 6: Thriving Beyond Heartbreak

Heartbreak, as painful as it is, offers an unexpected gift: the opportunity to start anew. It challenges you to reevaluate what matters most, to reconnect with your inner strength, and to build a life that aligns with your values and dreams. Thriving beyond heartbreak is not about forgetting what happened—it's about integrating those experiences into your story and using them as a foundation for growth.

This chapter is your guide to rediscovering joy, gratitude, self-love, and purpose. It's about taking the lessons heartbreak has taught you and applying them to create a life filled with authenticity, resilience, and connection.

Embracing Your New Normal

After heartbreak, life changes. The routines you shared with your partner, the dreams you built together, and even your sense of identity may feel like they've been uprooted. Accepting this "new normal" can be one of the hardest steps in the healing process.

- **Reflection Prompt:** What aspects of your life feel different since your heartbreak? How can you adjust to these changes while maintaining your sense of self?

Finding Peace in the Present

Thriving begins with grounding yourself in the present moment. Instead of fixating on what you've lost or worrying about the future, focus on what's happening right now. Mindfulness practices, such as meditation or deep breathing, can help you find peace amid uncertainty.

- **Practical Exercise:** Spend five minutes each morning practicing mindfulness. Sit in a quiet space, close your eyes, and focus on your breath. If your mind wanders, gently bring it back to the present.
- **Cultural Insight:** In many African traditions, mindfulness is woven into daily rituals, such as prayer, storytelling, or communal meals. Reconnecting with these practices can be a powerful way to find balance (American Psychological Association, 2021).

Discovering Joy and Gratitude

One of the most transformative steps in thriving is shifting your focus from what was lost to what can be gained. Joy and gratitude are not just emotions—they're practices that can reframe how you see the world.

Reclaiming Joy

Joy doesn't always come easily after heartbreak, but it can be rediscovered in small, everyday moments. Whether it's laughing with friends, listening to music, or watching the sunrise, these moments remind you that life still holds beauty.

- **Personal Insight:** For me, joy came in unexpected places. A walk in the park, a favorite childhood song, or a heartfelt conversation reminded me that happiness didn't have to be grand—it could be found in the little things.

Practicing Gratitude

Gratitude shifts your perspective, helping you focus on what you have rather than what you've lost. Studies show that practicing gratitude can improve mental health, increase resilience, and strengthen relationships (National Institutes of Health, 2020).

- **Practical Exercise:** Each night, write down three things you're grateful for. They don't have to be big—something as simple as a kind word from a friend or a good cup of coffee can count.

Rekindling Self-Love

Heartbreak often leaves us questioning our worth. Rekindling self-love means reminding yourself that you are deserving of care, kindness, and respect—both from others and from yourself.

Celebrating Your Strengths

Make a list of your strengths and accomplishments, no matter how small. This practice reinforces your sense of self-worth and reminds you of your resilience.

- **Practical Exercise:** Create a "self-love journal." Each day, write down one thing you like about yourself, whether it's a personality trait, a skill, or something you accomplished.

Addressing Self-Doubt

Self-doubt often creeps in after heartbreak, but it doesn't have to control you. Challenge negative thoughts with affirmations and reminders of your progress.

- **Example Affirmation:** "I am worthy of love and happiness, and I am capable of creating a life I'm proud of."

Redefining Love and Relationships

Thriving beyond heartbreak includes redefining what love means to you. Love is not limited to romantic partnerships—it also exists in friendships, family, and self-connection.

Entering Relationships with Clarity

If and when you're ready to pursue romantic relationships again, take time to reflect on what you truly want and need. Setting boundaries and communicating openly are key to building healthy connections.

- **Practical Advice:** Before entering a new relationship, make a list of your non-negotiables and values. This clarity will guide you toward a partnership that aligns with your growth.

Living with Purpose

Purpose is what gives our lives meaning. After heartbreak, reconnecting with your values and passions can help you build a future that feels authentic and fulfilling.

Using Your Pain as a Catalyst

Your experiences have given you unique insights and strength. Use them to inspire others, whether through mentoring, volunteering, or sharing your story.

- **Personal Insight:** Writing this book became my way of turning pain into purpose. It allowed me to process my experiences while creating something that could help others heal.

Setting Long-Term Goals

Long-term goals give you something to work toward, reminding you that your life is still full of potential.

- **Practical Exercise:** Write down one goal for each area of your life—personal, professional, and relational. Break each goal into smaller steps and celebrate your progress along the way.

Closing Thoughts for Chapter 6

Thriving beyond heartbreak isn't about erasing the past—it's about using it as a foundation for growth. By embracing your new normal, discovering joy, and living with purpose, you can create a life that reflects your strength, resilience, and vision for the future.

In the next chapter, we'll explore how to break barriers to mental health, addressing stigma and creating pathways to healing within the Black community.

Chapter 7: Breaking Barriers to Mental Health

Mental health is a topic that has long been surrounded by stigma, especially in Black communities. While strides have been made to raise awareness and improve access to care, barriers still exist that prevent many Black men from seeking the support they need. These barriers are not just cultural—they're systemic, historical, and deeply personal.

This chapter addresses the challenges Black men face when it comes to mental health, explores ways to overcome stigma, and highlights the importance of culturally competent care. It offers actionable steps to navigate the mental health system and foster healing within communities.

Addressing the Stigma in Black Communities

The stigma surrounding mental health in Black communities is deeply rooted in history and cultural norms. Generations of systemic oppression, combined with the need to appear resilient in the face of adversity, have contributed to a culture of silence around emotional struggles.

The Historical Context

The legacy of slavery, segregation, and systemic racism has profoundly shaped how Black people view mental health. Historically, Black individuals were often denied access to adequate healthcare, including mental health services, leading to mistrust of medical institutions (American Psychological Association, 2021). Additionally, the stereotype of the "strong Black man" has perpetuated the idea that seeking help is a sign of weakness.

- **Cultural Insight:** In many Black families, mental health struggles are often dismissed with phrases like "pray about it" or "toughen up." While faith and resilience are valuable, they shouldn't replace professional care when needed.

The Role of Masculinity

Societal expectations around masculinity further complicate the issue. Black men are often taught to suppress their emotions and equate vulnerability with weakness. This mindset not only discourages seeking help but also isolates men who are struggling.

- **Reflection Prompt:** Think about a time when you felt pressured to hide your emotions. How did that experience affect you?

Overcoming Stigma Through Education and Advocacy

Breaking the stigma around mental health starts with education. By normalizing conversations about mental health and highlighting its importance, we can begin to dismantle the cultural barriers that keep Black men from seeking help.

- **Personal Insight:** When I first considered therapy, I hesitated because I worried about what others might think. But the more I learned about the benefits of mental health care, the more I realized that seeking help wasn't a weakness—it was an act of strength.
- **Practical Advice:** Start small. Share a mental health article or podcast with a friend or family member. Normalize discussions about therapy and self-care in your community.

Seeking Culturally Competent Care

One of the most significant challenges Black men face in the mental health system is finding providers who understand their unique experiences. Culturally competent care is essential for creating a safe and supportive therapeutic environment.

What Is Culturally Competent Care?

Culturally competent care involves providers who are trained to understand and respect the cultural backgrounds of their clients. For Black men, this means working with therapists who recognize the impact of systemic racism, generational trauma, and cultural norms on mental health.

- **Example Insight:** A study by the National Institute on Minority Health and Health Disparities found that patients who received care from culturally competent providers were more likely to feel understood and engaged in their treatment (National Institutes of Health, 2020).

How to Find the Right Provider

Finding a therapist who aligns with your needs may take time, but it's worth the effort. Here are some tips:

1. **Search for Specialists:** Look for therapists who specialize in working with men of color or those who have training in cultural competency.
2. **Ask Questions:** During an initial consultation, ask the therapist about their experience working with Black clients and their approach to addressing cultural issues.

3. **Use Trusted Resources:** Platforms like *Therapy for Black Men* and *Black Men Heal* offer directories and resources specifically for Black men.

The Role of Community and Peer Support

Healing doesn't have to happen in isolation. Building a network of supportive peers can make the mental health journey less intimidating and more empowering.

Finding Support Groups

Support groups offer a space to connect with others who share similar experiences. These groups provide not only emotional support but also a sense of belonging and understanding.

*   **Practical Advice:** Look for local or online support groups tailored to Black men. Many organizations now offer virtual options, making it easier to connect from anywhere.

Leveraging Faith and Spirituality

For many Black men, faith and spirituality are central to their lives. While prayer and spiritual practices are valuable, they can also complement professional mental health care.

- **Example Insight:** A 2021 study found that integrating spiritual practices into therapy improved outcomes for Black men who valued faith as part of their identity (American Psychological Association, 2021).

Creating Pathways to Healing in Communities

Breaking barriers to mental health is not just an individual effort—it's a collective one. Communities play a vital role in normalizing mental health care and supporting those who seek help.

Encouraging Open Dialogue

Creating spaces for open and honest conversations about mental health can break the silence that perpetuates stigma.

- **Action Step:** Host a mental health discussion in your community, whether at a church, school, or community center. Invite mental health professionals to share resources and insights.

Mentoring the Next Generation

Breaking barriers also means teaching younger generations that it's okay to seek help. By modeling vulnerability and prioritizing mental health, you can inspire others to do the same.

- **Personal Insight:** When I began sharing my mental health journey with my younger cousins, I saw how much it resonated with them. They started asking questions about therapy and expressing emotions they had previously bottled up.

Closing Thoughts for Chapter 7

Breaking barriers to mental health is a courageous act, one that requires challenging deeply ingrained beliefs and systems. By addressing stigma, seeking culturally competent care, and fostering community support, Black men can create a new narrative—one that prioritizes healing, resilience, and growth.

In the next chapter, we'll explore how to leave a legacy of resilience, transforming your pain into a message of hope for future generations.

Chapter 8: Leaving a Legacy of Resilience

Healing from heartbreak isn't just about mending the wounds of the present—it's about creating a future where emotional strength, self-awareness, and resilience become the norm. For Black men, leaving a legacy of resilience means transforming pain into power, breaking generational cycles, and inspiring others to embrace vulnerability and growth.

This chapter is about the long-term impact of your healing journey. It's about turning your personal story into a message of hope and empowerment for the people who look to you for guidance, whether they are your children, family members, or community.

Transforming Your Pain Into Purpose

Pain can be a powerful teacher. While it's tempting to move past it as quickly as possible, the lessons it holds can shape not only your growth but also the impact you have on others.

Sharing Your Story

One of the most powerful ways to leave a legacy of resilience is by sharing your story. Your experiences—both the struggles and the triumphs—have the potential to inspire and empower others.

- **Personal Insight:** Writing this book became my way of turning pain into purpose. It allowed me to process my heartbreak while creating a resource for others who may feel alone in their struggles. Sharing my story reminded me that my pain wasn't just mine—it was part of a larger journey of healing and connection.
- **Action Step:** Consider how you might share your story. This could be through writing, public speaking, mentoring, or even casual conversations with loved ones.

Becoming a Source of Hope

When you model resilience, you show others that healing is possible. Whether it's offering a listening ear, encouraging someone to seek help, or simply being honest about your own journey, your actions can inspire those around you.

- **Reflection Prompt:** Think about someone in your life who has looked to you for guidance. How might your healing journey impact them?

Inspiring Future Generations

Leaving a legacy of resilience isn't just about the present—it's about planting seeds for the future. By modeling healthy behaviors and breaking destructive cycles, you pave the way for future generations to live more freely and authentically.

Breaking the Cycle

Many of the patterns we inherit, such as emotional suppression or avoidance, are passed down unintentionally. By actively breaking these cycles, you create a new foundation for the people who come after you.

- **Practical Advice:** Make a list of the emotional habits or beliefs you want to leave behind. Then, write down the values and behaviors you want to pass on instead.
- **Example Insight:** One father I worked with decided to break the cycle of emotional distance he experienced growing up. By consistently telling his children, "I love you," and encouraging them to express their feelings, he created a home where vulnerability was celebrated, not suppressed.

Mentoring and Community Leadership

Future generations don't just learn from what you say—they learn from what you do. Becoming a mentor or leader in your community allows you to pass on the lessons you've learned while creating a ripple effect of positive change.

- **Practical Advice:** Volunteer at a local organization, coach a youth team, or offer to speak at schools or community centers about emotional health and resilience.

Redefining Strength for the Future

Strength is often defined as stoicism or toughness, but true strength lies in vulnerability, compassion, and the courage to grow. Redefining what strength means for Black men is an essential part of leaving a legacy of resilience.

- **Cultural Insight:** In African traditions, strength was often rooted in community, collaboration, and storytelling. Returning to these roots can help Black men redefine masculinity in ways that honor both individual and collective growth (Minority Health, 2022).
- **Action Step:** Start conversations with young men in your life about what strength means. Encourage them to see vulnerability as a source of power, not weakness.

Turning Pain Into a Message of Hope

Your pain doesn't have to define you, but it can shape the message you leave behind. By using your experiences to uplift others, you turn your struggles into a source of inspiration and hope.

Creating a Legacy of Growth

A legacy of resilience isn't about perfection—it's about progress. It's about showing that growth is possible, even in the face of adversity.

- **Reflection Prompt:** What do you want people to remember about you? How can your healing journey contribute to the legacy you leave behind?

Amplifying Your Impact

Consider ways to amplify your message, whether it's through social media, community events, or collaborations with organizations that align with your values. Every action, no matter how small, contributes to a larger movement of healing and empowerment.

Closing Reflections

Leaving a legacy of resilience is one of the most profound ways to honor your healing journey. It's about transforming your pain into purpose, breaking generational cycles, and inspiring others to do the same. By choosing to heal, you not only change your own life—you change the lives of everyone who follows in your footsteps.

As you close this chapter of your story, remember that healing is an ongoing journey. Continue to show up for yourself and others, and know that your resilience is a testament to your strength, courage, and capacity for growth.

Acknowledgments: Gratitude and Support

No journey is taken alone, and this book is no exception. The words you've read and the lessons I've shared are shaped by the people who have stood by me, inspired me, and shown me what love, resilience, and growth truly mean.

First and foremost, I want to thank my fiancée, **Angelic Jenkins**, whose patience, understanding, and unwavering love have been a beacon of light through the darkest moments of my life. Angelic, thank you for standing by me even when the path was uncertain. Your strength and support through our own breakups have shown me the depth of true love and forgiveness. You are my partner, my muse, and my constant reminder that healing is possible when two people choose to fight for one another.

To my family and friends, thank you for being my foundation. Your encouragement and belief in me have kept me grounded and focused, even when doubt crept in.

To every Black man who has shared his story with me—whether in a therapy session, a conversation, or a moment of vulnerability—thank you for trusting me with your truth. Your bravery and honesty inspired the heart of this book.

Finally, to the readers: thank you for taking this journey with me. It is my hope that these pages bring you light, healing, and a sense of connection. May you find the strength to heal and the courage to thrive, knowing that you are never alone.

Would you like to expand this further or adjust the tone? Let me know if there are additional people, groups, or organizations you'd like me to include in this section!

Resources for Healing and Growth

Healing is a journey, and having the right tools and support can make all the difference. This section provides resources designed to support Black men in their mental health, emotional well-being, and personal growth. Whether you're seeking professional help, looking for community, or searching for further reading, these resources can guide you on your path.

Mental Health Organizations

1. **Therapy for Black Men**
    a. A platform dedicated to breaking the stigma of therapy in Black communities by connecting Black men with culturally competent therapists.
    b. Website: https://therapyforblackmen.org

2. **Black Men Heal**

a. Offers free mental health services and tools tailored to Black men's unique needs, including virtual therapy and peer support programs.

b. Website: https://blackmenheal.org

3. **The Boris Lawrence Henson Foundation**

a. Founded by Taraji P. Henson, this foundation provides mental health resources specifically for the Black community, including scholarships for therapy services.

b. Website: https://borislhensonfoundation.org

Books and Articles

1. **"The Unapologetic Guide to Black Mental Health" by Rheeda Walker, PhD**

a. A comprehensive guide to understanding and prioritizing mental health in the Black community.

2. **"It Didn't Start with You: How Inherited Family Trauma Shapes Who We Are and How to End the Cycle" by Mark Wolynn**

a. Explores the concept of generational trauma and offers tools to break cycles of pain.

3. **"Between the World and Me" by Ta-Nehisi Coates**

a. A powerful reflection on race, identity, and resilience in America.

4. **American Psychological Association (APA) Articles**

a. Explore peer-reviewed articles on trauma, mental health stigma, and culturally competent care at https://www.apa.org.

Support Groups and Communities

1. **Brother You're on My Mind**

    a. An initiative by Omega Psi Phi Fraternity, Inc. to raise awareness of mental health

    challenges among Black men.

    b. Website: https://www.oppf.org

2. **My Brother's Keeper Alliance (MBK)**

    a. Founded by President Barack Obama, MBK supports young men of color by

    addressing barriers to opportunity and fostering mentorship.

    b. Website: https://www.obama.org/mbka

3. **National Alliance on Mental Illness (NAMI)**

    a. Provides education, support groups, and resources for individuals and families

    affected by mental illness.

    b. Website: https://www.nami.org

Crisis Hotlines and Immediate Support

1. **988 Suicide & Crisis Lifeline**

    a. A free, confidential 24/7 support line for those experiencing emotional distress or

    suicidal thoughts.

    b. Dial 988 (USA)

2. **Crisis Text Line**

    a. Text "HOME" to 741741 for free, 24/7 crisis support via text.

3. **National Alliance on Mental Illness (NAMI) Helpline**

a. Call 1-800-950-NAMI (6264) for information, resources, and support.

REFERENCES:

Introduction: Breaking the Silence

1. **Statistic:** "Nearly 64% of Black children grow up in single-parent households."

    a. **Source:** U.S. Census Bureau. (2020). *Household Composition by Race.* Retrieved from https://www.census.gov.

2. **Insight on suicide rates among Black men:**

    a. **Source:** Centers for Disease Control and Prevention (CDC). (2020). *Suicide Prevention: Black Population.* Retrieved from https://www.cdc.gov.

3. **Stigma surrounding mental health in Black communities:**

    a. **Source:** American Psychological Association. (2021). *The Importance of Culturally Competent Mental Health Care.* Retrieved from https://www.apa.org.

Chapter 1: Understanding Heartbreak

1. **Neuroscientific study linking emotional and physical pain:**

    a. **Source:** National Institutes of Health. (2018). *The Neurological Basis of Emotional Pain.* Retrieved from https://www.nih.gov.

2. **Example of generational wounds and inherited trauma:**

    a. **Source:** Wolynn, M. (2016). *It Didn't Start with You: How Inherited Family Trauma Shapes Who We Are and How to End the Cycle.*

3. **Discussion of societal pressures on Black men's emotions:**

    a. **Source:** Minority Health. (2022). *Mental and Behavioral Health: African Americans.* Retrieved from https://minorityhealth.hhs.gov.

Chapter 2: Steps Toward Healing

1. **Social support's impact on emotional recovery:**

    a. **Source:** Holt-Lunstad, J. (2017). *The Impact of Loneliness and Social Isolation on Mortality. Perspectives on Psychological Science, 10*(2), 227-237.

2. **Effectiveness of therapy, especially for Black men:**

    a. **Source:** Therapy for Black Men. (2023). *Breaking the Stigma of Therapy.* Retrieved from https://therapyforblackmen.org.

3. **Daily routines (e.g., journaling and exercise) for mental health improvement:**

    a. **Source:** National Institute on Mental Health. (2020). *The Benefits of Exercise on Mental Health.* Retrieved from https://www.nimh.nih.gov.

Chapter 3: Rebuilding Confidence and Purpose

1. **Redefining strength and self-worth after heartbreak:**

    a. **Source:** Coates, T.-N. (2015). *Between the World and Me.*

2. **Benefits of small, measurable goals on mental health:**

a. **Source:** American Psychological Association. (2021). *Building Resilience: A Guide for Individuals.* Retrieved from https://www.apa.org.

Chapter 4: Healing Relationships

1. **Impact of isolation on mental and physical health:**

    a. **Source:** Holt-Lunstad, J. (2017). *The Impact of Loneliness and Social Isolation on Mortality. Perspectives on Psychological Science, 10*(2), 227-237.

2. **Cultural norms affecting vulnerability in Black families:**

    a. **Source:** Minority Health. (2022). *Mental and Behavioral Health: African Americans.* Retrieved from https://minorityhealth.hhs.gov.

3. **Rebuilding trust and setting boundaries:**

    a. **Source:** Brown, B. (2012). *Daring Greatly: How the Courage to Be Vulnerable Transforms the Way We Live, Love, Parent, and Lead.*

Chapter 5: Breaking Generational Cycles of Pain

1. **Epigenetic research on inherited trauma:**

    a. **Source:** National Institutes of Health. (2018). *Epigenetics and Trauma Transmission.* Retrieved from https://www.nih.gov.

2. **Forgiveness and its role in emotional healing:**

    a. **Source:** Luskin, F. (2002). *Forgive for Good: A Proven Prescription for Health and Happiness.*

3. **Building new habits for emotional intelligence:**

   a. **Source:** Goleman, D. (1995). *Emotional Intelligence: Why It Can Matter More Than IQ.*

Chapter 6: Thriving Beyond Heartbreak

1. **Practicing mindfulness to embrace the present:**

   a. **Source:** Kabat-Zinn, J. (1990). *Full Catastrophe Living: Using the Wisdom of Your Body and Mind to Face Stress, Pain, and Illness.*

2. **Gratitude's positive effects on mental health:**

   a. **Source:** Emmons, R. A., & McCullough, M. E. (2003). *Counting Blessings Versus Burdens: An Experimental Investigation of Gratitude and Subjective Well-Being in Daily Life. Journal of Personality and Social Psychology, 84*(2), 377-389.

Chapter 7: Breaking Barriers to Mental Health

1. **Importance of culturally competent care:**

   a. **Source:** Therapy for Black Men. (2023). *Breaking the Stigma of Therapy.* Retrieved from https://therapyforblackmen.org.

2. **Integrating spirituality into therapy:**

   a. **Source:** American Psychological Association. (2021). *Faith and Mental Health in Black Communities.* Retrieved from https://www.apa.org.

Chapter 8: Leaving a Legacy of Resilience

1. **Modeling resilience for future generations:**

   a. **Source:** Wolynn, M. (2016). *It Didn't Start with You: How Inherited Family Trauma Shapes Who We Are and How to End the Cycle.*

2. **Strengthening communities through mentorship:**

   a. **Source:** My Brother's Keeper Alliance. (2023). *Empowering Young Men of Color.* Retrieved from https://www.obama.org/mbka.

Expanded References Section

1. American Psychological Association. (2021). *The Importance of Culturally Competent Mental Health Care.* Retrieved from https://www.apa.org.

2. Brown, B. (2012). *Daring Greatly: How the Courage to Be Vulnerable Transforms the Way We Live, Love, Parent, and Lead.*

3. Centers for Disease Control and Prevention (CDC). (2020). *Suicide Prevention: Black Population.* Retrieved from https://www.cdc.gov.

4. Coates, T.-N. (2015). *Between the World and Me.*

5. Emmons, R. A., & McCullough, M. E. (2003). *Counting Blessings Versus Burdens: An Experimental Investigation of Gratitude and Subjective Well-Being in Daily Life. Journal of Personality and Social Psychology, 84*(2), 377-389.

6. Goleman, D. (1995). *Emotional Intelligence: Why It Can Matter More Than IQ.*

7. Holt-Lunstad, J. (2017). *The Impact of Loneliness and Social Isolation on Mortality. Perspectives on Psychological Science, 10*(2), 227-237.

8. Kabat-Zinn, J. (1990). *Full Catastrophe Living: Using the Wisdom of Your Body and Mind to Face Stress, Pain, and Illness.*

9. Luskin, F. (2002). *Forgive for Good: A Proven Prescription for Health and Happiness.*

10. Minority Health. (2022). *Mental and Behavioral Health: African Americans.* Retrieved from https://minorityhealth.hhs.gov.

11. My Brother's Keeper Alliance. (2023). *Empowering Young Men of Color.* Retrieved from https://www.obama.org/mbka.

12. National Institutes of Health. (2018). *Epigenetics and Trauma Transmission.* Retrieved from https://www.nih.gov.

13. Therapy for Black Men. (2023). *Breaking the Stigma of Therapy.* Retrieved from https://therapyforblackmen.org.

14. U.S. Census Bureau. (2020). *Household Composition by Race.* Retrieved from https://www.census.gov.

15. Wolynn, M. (2016). *It Didn't Start with You: How Inherited Family Trauma Shapes Who We Are and How to End the Cycle.*

www.ingramcontent.com/pod-product-compliance
Lightning Source LLC
Chambersburg PA
CBHW051915250726
48659CB00002B/656